50 Mexican Chicken Dishes

By: Kelly Johnson

Table of Contents

- Chicken Enchiladas
- Pollo Asado
- Chicken Tacos
- Chicken Tamales
- Chicken Fajitas
- Chicken Quesadillas
- Arroz con Pollo (Chicken with Rice)
- Chicken Mole
- Chicken Tortilla Soup
- Pollo a la Mexicana
- Chicken Chile Verde
- Tostadas de Pollo
- Chicken Sopes
- Chicken and Cheese Chile Rellenos
- Pollo con Papas (Chicken with Potatoes)
- Mexican Chicken Casserole
- Pollo Pibil (Yucatan-style Chicken)
- Chicken Picadillo
- Mexican Chicken Salad
- Chicken in Red Chile Sauce
- Pollo al Ajillo (Garlic Chicken)
- Chicken Flautas
- Chicken Carnitas
- Chicken Fajita Bowls
- Chicken Chilaquiles
- Chicken and Rice Soup (Caldo de Pollo)
- Chicken Tortas
- Pollo a la Crema
- Spicy Chicken Tostadas
- Chicken and Black Bean Enchiladas
- Pollo con Mole Poblano
- Chicken Pozole
- Grilled Chicken with Cilantro and Lime
- Chicken Empanadas
- Chicken Tamale Pie

- Chicken and Corn Chili
- Mexican Chicken and Avocado Salad
- Chicken Empanadas with Salsa Verde
- Baked Chicken with Mexican Spices
- Chicken and Bean Burritos
- Pollo en Salsa Roja
- Chicken Fajita Skillet
- Chicken and Zucchini Tacos
- Baked Chicken with Mole Sauce
- Chicken Chile Rellenos Casserole
- Chicken and Spinach Enchiladas
- Pollo en Salsa de Tamarindo (Tamarind Chicken)
- Chicken Salsas with Tortillas
- Chicken and Pineapple Tacos
- Chicken Taco Salad

Chicken Enchiladas

Ingredients:

- 2 cups cooked and shredded chicken
- 1 cup enchilada sauce
- 10-12 corn tortillas
- 1 cup shredded cheese (cheddar or Mexican blend)
- 1/2 cup diced onions
- 1/2 cup sour cream (optional for topping)
- 1 tbsp olive oil
- 1 tsp cumin
- 1 tsp garlic powder
- 1 tsp chili powder
- Salt and pepper to taste

Instructions:

1. Preheat the oven to 375°F (190°C).
2. In a bowl, mix the shredded chicken with cumin, garlic powder, chili powder, salt, and pepper.
3. Heat the tortillas in a pan with a little olive oil until soft and warm.
4. Pour a little enchilada sauce into a baking dish.
5. Take each tortilla and fill it with the chicken mixture, then roll it up tightly.
6. Place the rolled tortillas in the baking dish, cover with remaining enchilada sauce, and top with shredded cheese and onions.
7. Bake for 20-25 minutes until the cheese is melted and bubbly.
8. Serve with sour cream if desired.

Pollo Asado

Ingredients:

- 4 chicken thighs (or breasts)
- 2 tbsp olive oil
- Juice of 2 limes
- 3 cloves garlic, minced
- 1 tsp chili powder
- 1 tsp cumin
- 1 tsp paprika
- 1/2 tsp oregano
- Salt and pepper to taste

Instructions:

1. In a bowl, mix olive oil, lime juice, garlic, chili powder, cumin, paprika, oregano, salt, and pepper.
2. Coat the chicken thighs in the marinade and refrigerate for at least 1 hour (or overnight for deeper flavor).
3. Preheat a grill or skillet over medium-high heat.
4. Grill the chicken for 6-7 minutes per side, or until the internal temperature reaches 165°F (75°C).
5. Serve with rice, tortillas, or your favorite sides.

Chicken Tacos

Ingredients:

- 2 cups cooked and shredded chicken
- 1 tbsp taco seasoning
- 1/2 cup chicken broth
- 8-10 soft or hard taco shells
- Toppings: lettuce, tomatoes, cheese, sour cream, salsa, cilantro

Instructions:

1. In a saucepan, combine shredded chicken, taco seasoning, and chicken broth. Simmer over medium heat for 5-10 minutes until the chicken is heated through and coated in the sauce.
2. Heat taco shells according to package instructions.
3. Assemble tacos by filling the shells with the seasoned chicken and your choice of toppings.
4. Serve immediately.

Chicken Tamales

Ingredients:

- 2 cups cooked and shredded chicken
- 1 cup enchilada sauce
- 2 cups masa harina (corn dough)
- 1/2 cup chicken broth
- 1/2 cup vegetable oil
- 1 tsp cumin
- 1 tsp garlic powder
- 10-12 corn husks (soaked in warm water)

Instructions:

1. In a bowl, mix the shredded chicken with enchilada sauce, cumin, and garlic powder. Set aside.
2. In another bowl, mix masa harina, chicken broth, vegetable oil, and a pinch of salt until smooth.
3. Take a soaked corn husk, spread a small amount of masa dough on it, and then add a spoonful of chicken filling.
4. Roll the tamale tightly, folding in the sides of the husk.
5. Steam the tamales in a large steamer for 1-1.5 hours, or until the masa is fully cooked.
6. Serve with salsa or crema.

Chicken Fajitas

Ingredients:

- 4 chicken breasts or thighs, sliced into strips
- 1 onion, sliced
- 2 bell peppers, sliced
- 2 tbsp fajita seasoning
- 1 tbsp olive oil
- 1 tbsp lime juice
- 8 small flour tortillas
- Toppings: guacamole, sour cream, salsa, cilantro

Instructions:

1. Heat olive oil in a large skillet over medium-high heat.
2. Add the sliced chicken and cook until browned, about 5-7 minutes.
3. Add the onions, bell peppers, and fajita seasoning, and cook for another 5-7 minutes, stirring occasionally.
4. Squeeze lime juice over the chicken and veggies.
5. Warm the tortillas in a pan or microwave.
6. Serve the fajita filling with tortillas and your choice of toppings.

Chicken Quesadillas

Ingredients:

- 2 cups cooked and shredded chicken
- 1 cup shredded cheese (cheddar or Mexican blend)
- 4 flour tortillas
- 1/4 cup chopped onions
- 1/4 cup chopped cilantro
- 1 tbsp olive oil or butter

Instructions:

1. Heat a pan over medium heat and brush with olive oil or butter.
2. Place a tortilla in the pan, sprinkle with cheese, chicken, onions, and cilantro, and top with a second tortilla.
3. Cook for 2-3 minutes on each side until the cheese is melted and the tortillas are golden brown.
4. Slice into wedges and serve with salsa or sour cream.

Arroz con Pollo (Chicken with Rice)

Ingredients:

- 4 chicken thighs or breasts, bone-in
- 1 cup long-grain rice
- 1 onion, chopped
- 1 bell pepper, chopped
- 2 cloves garlic, minced
- 1 can diced tomatoes
- 2 cups chicken broth
- 1 tsp cumin
- 1 tsp paprika
- Salt and pepper to taste

Instructions:

1. In a large pot, heat oil and brown the chicken pieces on both sides. Remove and set aside.
2. In the same pot, sauté onions, bell pepper, and garlic until softened.
3. Add the rice, cumin, paprika, salt, and pepper, and stir to coat.
4. Add diced tomatoes, chicken broth, and the browned chicken.
5. Bring to a boil, then reduce the heat to low and cover. Simmer for 20-25 minutes, or until the rice is tender and the chicken is cooked through.
6. Serve hot.

Chicken Mole

Ingredients:

- 4 chicken thighs or breasts
- 1/2 cup mole sauce (store-bought or homemade)
- 1 cup chicken broth
- 1/4 cup sesame seeds (for garnish)
- 1 tbsp olive oil

Instructions:

1. Heat olive oil in a large skillet over medium heat.
2. Brown the chicken pieces on both sides, about 5-7 minutes per side.
3. Add mole sauce and chicken broth to the skillet, and bring to a simmer.
4. Cover and cook for 30-35 minutes, or until the chicken is fully cooked.
5. Garnish with sesame seeds and serve with rice or tortillas.

Chicken Tortilla Soup

Ingredients:

- 2 cups cooked and shredded chicken
- 1 can diced tomatoes
- 1 onion, chopped
- 2 cloves garlic, minced
- 4 cups chicken broth
- 1 tsp cumin
- 1 tsp chili powder
- 1/2 tsp oregano
- Tortilla chips (for serving)
- Toppings: avocado, cilantro, cheese, sour cream

Instructions:

1. In a large pot, sauté onions and garlic until softened.
2. Add diced tomatoes, chicken broth, shredded chicken, cumin, chili powder, and oregano. Bring to a boil.
3. Reduce heat and simmer for 15-20 minutes.
4. Serve the soup with crushed tortilla chips and your choice of toppings.

Pollo a la Mexicana

Ingredients:

- 4 chicken breasts, cut into cubes
- 2 tomatoes, diced
- 1 onion, diced
- 2 cloves garlic, minced
- 1 jalapeño, minced (optional for heat)
- 1/2 cup chicken broth
- 1 tbsp vegetable oil
- 1 tsp cumin
- 1 tsp paprika
- Salt and pepper to taste
- Fresh cilantro, chopped for garnish

Instructions:

1. Heat oil in a large skillet over medium heat. Add the diced chicken and cook until browned on all sides.
2. Add the onion, garlic, and jalapeño to the skillet, and sauté until softened.
3. Stir in the diced tomatoes, chicken broth, cumin, paprika, salt, and pepper. Simmer for 10-15 minutes until the sauce thickens and the chicken is fully cooked.
4. Garnish with fresh cilantro and serve with rice or tortillas.

Chicken Chile Verde

Ingredients:

- 4 chicken breasts, cooked and shredded
- 1 lb tomatillos, husked and washed
- 2 poblano peppers
- 1 onion, chopped
- 2 cloves garlic
- 1 jalapeño, seeded (optional)
- 2 cups chicken broth
- 1 tsp cumin
- Salt and pepper to taste
- Fresh cilantro, chopped for garnish

Instructions:

1. Roast the tomatillos and poblano peppers on a hot skillet or grill until charred. Peel the skins off the peppers and remove the seeds.
2. In a blender, combine the roasted tomatillos, poblano peppers, garlic, onion, and jalapeño. Blend until smooth.
3. Pour the sauce into a pot, add the shredded chicken, chicken broth, cumin, salt, and pepper. Simmer for 20 minutes.
4. Garnish with cilantro and serve with warm tortillas or rice.

Tostadas de Pollo

Ingredients:

- 2 cups cooked and shredded chicken
- 8 tostada shells
- 1/2 cup refried beans
- 1/2 cup shredded lettuce
- 1/2 cup diced tomatoes
- 1/2 cup shredded cheese
- 1/4 cup sour cream
- Salsa for topping

Instructions:

1. Heat the tostada shells in the oven or on a skillet until crispy.
2. Spread a layer of refried beans on each tostada shell.
3. Top with shredded chicken, lettuce, tomatoes, cheese, sour cream, and salsa.
4. Serve immediately for a delicious and crunchy meal.

Chicken Sopes

Ingredients:

- 2 cups cooked and shredded chicken
- 10-12 small sopes (thick corn tortillas)
- 1/2 cup refried beans
- 1/2 cup shredded lettuce
- 1/2 cup diced tomatoes
- 1/4 cup sour cream
- Salsa for topping
- 1/2 cup crumbled queso fresco

Instructions:

1. Heat the sopes on a skillet until they are crispy on the edges but still soft in the center.
2. Spread a layer of refried beans on each sope.
3. Top with shredded chicken, lettuce, tomatoes, sour cream, salsa, and queso fresco.
4. Serve with extra salsa and a squeeze of lime.

Chicken and Cheese Chile Rellenos

Ingredients:

- 4 large poblano peppers
- 2 cups cooked and shredded chicken
- 1 cup shredded cheese (cheddar or Mexican blend)
- 1/4 cup chopped onion
- 1/4 cup chopped cilantro
- 1 egg, beaten
- 1/2 cup flour
- Salt and pepper to taste
- Vegetable oil for frying

Instructions:

1. Roast the poblano peppers over an open flame or under a broiler until charred. Peel off the skins and remove the seeds.
2. Stuff each pepper with shredded chicken, cheese, onion, and cilantro.
3. In a shallow dish, combine the flour, salt, and pepper. Dip each stuffed pepper into the flour, then into the beaten egg.
4. Heat oil in a frying pan over medium heat. Fry each stuffed pepper until golden brown and crispy.
5. Serve with rice or beans and a drizzle of salsa.

Pollo con Papas (Chicken with Potatoes)

Ingredients:

- 4 chicken thighs or breasts
- 4 medium potatoes, peeled and cubed
- 1 onion, chopped
- 2 cloves garlic, minced
- 1 tsp cumin
- 1 tsp paprika
- 1/2 tsp oregano
- 1 cup chicken broth
- 2 tbsp olive oil
- Salt and pepper to taste

Instructions:

1. Heat olive oil in a large skillet over medium heat. Brown the chicken on both sides and remove from the skillet.
2. In the same skillet, add onions and garlic, and sauté until softened.
3. Add the cubed potatoes, cumin, paprika, oregano, salt, and pepper. Stir to combine.
4. Return the chicken to the skillet and pour in the chicken broth. Cover and simmer for 25-30 minutes, or until the chicken is cooked and the potatoes are tender.
5. Serve hot with a side of vegetables.

Mexican Chicken Casserole

Ingredients:

- 2 cups cooked and shredded chicken
- 1 can diced tomatoes
- 1 can green chilies
- 1 cup frozen corn
- 1/2 cup chopped onion
- 2 cups shredded cheese (cheddar or Mexican blend)
- 1 cup sour cream
- 1/2 cup mayonnaise
- 1 tbsp taco seasoning
- 1/2 cup crushed tortilla chips (for topping)

Instructions:

1. Preheat the oven to 350°F (175°C).
2. In a large mixing bowl, combine shredded chicken, diced tomatoes, green chilies, corn, onion, cheese, sour cream, mayonnaise, and taco seasoning.
3. Transfer the mixture to a greased casserole dish and top with crushed tortilla chips.
4. Bake for 25-30 minutes until the casserole is hot and bubbly.
5. Serve with a side of rice or a simple salad.

Pollo Pibil (Yucatan-style Chicken)

Ingredients:

- 4 chicken thighs, bone-in
- 1/4 cup achiote paste
- 1/4 cup orange juice
- 1/4 cup lime juice
- 1/4 cup vinegar
- 1/2 tsp cumin
- 1/2 tsp oregano
- 2 cloves garlic, minced
- 2 banana leaves (optional for wrapping)
- Salt and pepper to taste

Instructions:

1. In a bowl, combine achiote paste, orange juice, lime juice, vinegar, cumin, oregano, garlic, salt, and pepper. Mix well to form a marinade.
2. Coat the chicken thighs in the marinade and refrigerate for at least 2 hours (or overnight for deeper flavor).
3. If using banana leaves, heat them over an open flame until softened. Wrap the marinated chicken in the leaves.
4. Steam the wrapped chicken over medium heat for 45 minutes or until fully cooked.
5. Serve with rice and tortillas.

Chicken Picadillo

Ingredients:

- 2 cups cooked and shredded chicken
- 1/2 cup raisins
- 1/4 cup olives, chopped
- 1/2 cup diced potatoes
- 1/2 cup diced tomatoes
- 1/2 cup chopped onion
- 1/2 tsp cumin
- 1/2 tsp cinnamon
- 1/4 cup chicken broth
- Salt and pepper to taste

Instructions:

1. Heat oil in a skillet over medium heat. Add onions and sauté until softened.
2. Add diced potatoes, cumin, cinnamon, and a pinch of salt. Cook until the potatoes are golden brown.
3. Stir in the cooked chicken, raisins, olives, diced tomatoes, and chicken broth. Simmer for 10-15 minutes, until the flavors meld and the potatoes are tender.
4. Serve hot with rice or tortillas.

Mexican Chicken Salad

Ingredients:

- 2 cups cooked and shredded chicken
- 1/2 cup corn kernels (fresh or frozen)
- 1/2 cup black beans, drained and rinsed
- 1 cup chopped Romaine lettuce
- 1/2 cup diced tomatoes
- 1/4 cup red onion, thinly sliced
- 1/2 avocado, diced
- 1/4 cup fresh cilantro, chopped
- 1/4 cup lime juice
- 2 tbsp olive oil
- Salt and pepper to taste

Instructions:

1. In a large bowl, combine shredded chicken, corn, black beans, lettuce, tomatoes, red onion, avocado, and cilantro.
2. In a separate small bowl, whisk together lime juice, olive oil, salt, and pepper.
3. Pour the dressing over the salad and toss gently to combine.
4. Serve immediately as a light and refreshing meal.

Chicken in Red Chile Sauce

Ingredients:

- 4 chicken thighs or breasts
- 4 dried ancho chiles, stemmed and seeded
- 2 dried guajillo chiles, stemmed and seeded
- 2 cloves garlic
- 1/2 onion, chopped
- 1 cup chicken broth
- 1 tsp cumin
- 1 tsp paprika
- Salt and pepper to taste
- 2 tbsp vegetable oil

Instructions:

1. Toast the dried chiles in a hot skillet for a few seconds to release their flavors, then soak them in warm water for 15-20 minutes.
2. Blend the soaked chiles, garlic, onion, cumin, paprika, and chicken broth into a smooth sauce.
3. Heat oil in a skillet over medium heat. Season the chicken with salt and pepper, and brown it on both sides.
4. Pour the red chile sauce over the chicken and simmer for 20-30 minutes until the chicken is fully cooked.
5. Serve with rice or tortillas.

Pollo al Ajillo (Garlic Chicken)

Ingredients:

- 4 chicken thighs or breasts
- 8 cloves garlic, minced
- 1/4 cup olive oil
- 1/2 cup white wine
- 1 tsp thyme
- 1 tsp paprika
- Salt and pepper to taste
- Fresh parsley, chopped for garnish

Instructions:

1. Heat olive oil in a large skillet over medium heat. Add the chicken and cook until browned on both sides. Remove and set aside.
2. In the same skillet, add minced garlic and sauté until fragrant.
3. Pour in the white wine and scrape up any browned bits from the pan. Stir in thyme, paprika, salt, and pepper.
4. Return the chicken to the skillet, cover, and cook for another 20-30 minutes, or until the chicken is cooked through.
5. Garnish with fresh parsley and serve with a side of vegetables or potatoes.

Chicken Flautas

Ingredients:

- 2 cups cooked and shredded chicken
- 1/2 cup shredded cheese (cheddar or Mexican blend)
- 10 small corn tortillas
- Vegetable oil for frying
- Salsa, sour cream, and guacamole for serving

Instructions:

1. Heat the tortillas on a dry skillet until soft. Place a spoonful of shredded chicken and cheese on each tortilla.
2. Roll up each tortilla tightly to form a flauta.
3. Heat oil in a large skillet over medium heat. Fry the flautas until golden and crispy, turning to cook evenly on all sides.
4. Drain the excess oil on paper towels and serve with salsa, sour cream, and guacamole.

Chicken Carnitas

Ingredients:

- 4 chicken thighs, skinless and boneless
- 1 onion, chopped
- 2 cloves garlic, minced
- 1 orange, juiced
- 1 tsp cumin
- 1 tsp oregano
- Salt and pepper to taste
- 1/4 cup vegetable oil
- Corn tortillas for serving

Instructions:

1. Season the chicken thighs with cumin, oregano, salt, and pepper.
2. Heat vegetable oil in a large skillet over medium heat. Brown the chicken on both sides, then remove and set aside.
3. In the same skillet, sauté the onion and garlic until soft.
4. Return the chicken to the skillet, add orange juice, and cover. Simmer for 25-30 minutes until the chicken is tender and easy to shred.
5. Shred the chicken and serve with warm corn tortillas and your favorite toppings.

Chicken Fajita Bowls

Ingredients:

- 2 chicken breasts, sliced into strips
- 1 red bell pepper, sliced
- 1 green bell pepper, sliced
- 1 onion, sliced
- 1 tbsp fajita seasoning
- 1 tbsp olive oil
- 2 cups cooked rice (white or brown)
- 1/2 cup salsa
- 1/2 cup sour cream
- Fresh cilantro for garnish

Instructions:

1. Heat olive oil in a skillet over medium heat. Add the chicken strips and fajita seasoning. Cook until browned and cooked through.
2. Add the bell peppers and onion, and sauté until tender.
3. Serve the chicken and vegetable mixture over a bed of rice. Top with salsa, sour cream, and cilantro.
4. Serve with lime wedges on the side.

Chicken Chilaquiles

Ingredients:

- 2 cups cooked and shredded chicken
- 8-10 tortilla chips (or homemade fried tortilla strips)
- 1 cup green enchilada sauce
- 1/2 cup shredded cheese
- 2 eggs, scrambled (optional)
- 1/4 cup diced onions
- 1/4 cup fresh cilantro, chopped
- Salsa and sour cream for serving

Instructions:

1. Heat the green enchilada sauce in a skillet over medium heat.
2. Add the tortilla chips and cook for a few minutes until they soften and absorb the sauce.
3. Stir in the shredded chicken, and cook until heated through.
4. If using, scramble the eggs in a separate pan and add them to the chilaquiles.
5. Top with cheese, onions, cilantro, salsa, and sour cream. Serve immediately.

Chicken and Rice Soup (Caldo de Pollo)

Ingredients:

- 4 chicken thighs or breasts, bone-in
- 1 cup rice, rinsed
- 1 carrot, sliced
- 1 zucchini, diced
- 1 onion, chopped
- 2 cloves garlic, minced
- 1 tsp cumin
- 1/2 tsp oregano
- 6 cups chicken broth
- Fresh cilantro, chopped for garnish
- Lime wedges for serving

Instructions:

1. In a large pot, combine chicken, rice, carrot, zucchini, onion, garlic, cumin, oregano, and chicken broth.
2. Bring the mixture to a boil, then reduce the heat and simmer for 30-40 minutes, until the chicken is cooked through and the rice is tender.
3. Remove the chicken, shred it, and return it to the pot.
4. Garnish with fresh cilantro and serve with lime wedges.

Chicken Tortas

Ingredients:

- 2 cups cooked and shredded chicken
- 4 bolillo rolls (Mexican bread rolls)
- 1/4 cup mayonnaise
- 1/4 cup salsa
- 1/2 avocado, sliced
- 1/4 cup sliced onion
- 1/4 cup fresh cilantro, chopped

Instructions:

1. Slice the bolillo rolls in half and toast them until golden.
2. Mix mayonnaise and salsa together and spread it on the inside of each roll.
3. Layer the shredded chicken, avocado, onion, and cilantro in the rolls.
4. Close the tortas and serve with a side of chips or a salad.

Pollo a la Crema

Ingredients:

- 4 chicken breasts
- 1 cup heavy cream
- 1/2 cup chicken broth
- 1/4 cup butter
- 1/2 onion, chopped
- 2 cloves garlic, minced
- 1 tsp cumin
- Salt and pepper to taste
- Fresh cilantro, chopped for garnish

Instructions:

1. In a skillet, melt butter over medium heat. Add the chicken breasts and cook until browned on both sides. Remove and set aside.
2. In the same skillet, sauté onion and garlic until soft.
3. Pour in the chicken broth and heavy cream, and stir in cumin, salt, and pepper.
4. Return the chicken to the skillet and simmer for 20-25 minutes, or until the chicken is fully cooked and the sauce thickens.
5. Garnish with fresh cilantro and serve with rice or tortillas.

Spicy Chicken Tostadas

Ingredients:

- 2 cups cooked and shredded chicken
- 1 tbsp chili powder
- 1 tsp cumin
- 1/2 tsp paprika
- 1 tbsp hot sauce (optional)
- 8 tostada shells
- 1/2 cup refried beans
- 1/2 cup shredded lettuce
- 1/4 cup diced tomatoes
- 1/4 cup chopped onions
- 1/2 avocado, sliced
- Salsa, sour cream, and cilantro for garnish

Instructions:

1. In a bowl, toss the shredded chicken with chili powder, cumin, paprika, and hot sauce (if using).
2. Spread a thin layer of refried beans on each tostada shell.
3. Top with the seasoned chicken, lettuce, tomatoes, onions, and avocado.
4. Garnish with salsa, sour cream, and cilantro.
5. Serve immediately as a crunchy, spicy appetizer or meal.

Chicken and Black Bean Enchiladas

Ingredients:

- 2 cups cooked and shredded chicken
- 1 cup black beans, drained and rinsed
- 1 cup enchilada sauce
- 8 small corn tortillas
- 1 cup shredded cheese (Mexican blend)
- 1/2 cup sour cream
- Fresh cilantro for garnish

Instructions:

1. Preheat the oven to 375°F (190°C).
2. Mix shredded chicken and black beans together. Add 1/2 cup of enchilada sauce and stir to combine.
3. Warm the tortillas and spoon the chicken and bean mixture into each one. Roll them up and place them in a baking dish.
4. Pour the remaining enchilada sauce over the rolled tortillas and sprinkle with cheese.
5. Bake for 20 minutes or until the cheese is melted and bubbly.
6. Serve with a dollop of sour cream and fresh cilantro on top.

Pollo con Mole Poblano

Ingredients:

- 4 chicken thighs or breasts
- 1/2 cup mole poblano paste
- 1/2 cup chicken broth
- 1 tbsp vegetable oil
- 1/4 cup chopped onion
- 2 cloves garlic, minced
- 1 tsp cumin
- 1/4 tsp cinnamon
- Salt and pepper to taste

Instructions:

1. In a skillet, heat oil over medium heat. Season the chicken with salt and pepper and brown on both sides.
2. Remove the chicken and set aside. In the same skillet, sauté onions and garlic until fragrant.
3. Add the mole paste, chicken broth, cumin, and cinnamon, and stir until smooth.
4. Return the chicken to the skillet and simmer for 20-25 minutes, or until the chicken is fully cooked and tender.
5. Serve with rice or tortillas, garnished with fresh cilantro.

Chicken Pozole

Ingredients:

- 2 cups cooked chicken, shredded
- 2 cups hominy (canned or dried)
- 1 onion, chopped
- 2 cloves garlic, minced
- 1 tbsp chili powder
- 1 tsp cumin
- 1/2 tsp oregano
- 4 cups chicken broth
- 1 tbsp lime juice
- Sliced radishes, shredded cabbage, and cilantro for garnish

Instructions:

1. In a large pot, combine the chicken, hominy, onion, garlic, chili powder, cumin, oregano, and chicken broth.
2. Bring the mixture to a boil, then reduce the heat and simmer for 30 minutes.
3. Stir in lime juice, and adjust seasoning with salt and pepper.
4. Serve the pozole in bowls and garnish with radishes, shredded cabbage, and cilantro.

Grilled Chicken with Cilantro and Lime

Ingredients:

- 4 chicken breasts
- 1/4 cup fresh cilantro, chopped
- 2 tbsp lime juice
- 1 tbsp olive oil
- 2 cloves garlic, minced
- 1 tsp cumin
- Salt and pepper to taste

Instructions:

1. In a bowl, whisk together cilantro, lime juice, olive oil, garlic, cumin, salt, and pepper.
2. Marinate the chicken breasts in the cilantro-lime mixture for at least 30 minutes.
3. Preheat the grill to medium-high heat and grill the chicken for 6-8 minutes per side, or until cooked through.
4. Serve with a side of grilled vegetables or a fresh salad.

Chicken Empanadas

Ingredients:

- 2 cups cooked and shredded chicken
- 1/2 cup diced onion
- 1/2 cup diced bell pepper
- 1/4 cup tomato paste
- 1/2 tsp cumin
- 1/4 tsp paprika
- Salt and pepper to taste
- 1 package empanada dough (or homemade dough)
- 1 egg (for egg wash)

Instructions:

1. Preheat the oven to 375°F (190°C).
2. In a skillet, sauté onions and bell peppers until soft. Add the tomato paste, cumin, paprika, salt, and pepper, and cook for 2-3 minutes.
3. Stir in the shredded chicken and cook for another 5 minutes until everything is combined.
4. Roll out the empanada dough and spoon some of the chicken mixture into the center of each circle.
5. Fold the dough over and crimp the edges to seal. Brush the empanadas with a beaten egg.
6. Place the empanadas on a baking sheet and bake for 20 minutes, or until golden brown.
7. Serve with salsa or sour cream for dipping.

Chicken Tamale Pie

Ingredients:

- 2 cups cooked and shredded chicken
- 1 cup cornmeal
- 1 cup chicken broth
- 1 cup shredded cheese
- 1 can diced tomatoes with green chilies
- 1 tsp chili powder
- 1/2 tsp cumin
- Salt and pepper to taste
- Fresh cilantro for garnish

Instructions:

1. Preheat the oven to 350°F (175°C).
2. In a skillet, combine the shredded chicken, diced tomatoes, chili powder, cumin, salt, and pepper. Cook until heated through.
3. In a separate pot, bring chicken broth to a boil, then stir in cornmeal and cook until thickened.
4. Layer the chicken mixture in the bottom of a baking dish, then top with the cornmeal mixture and shredded cheese.
5. Bake for 20 minutes or until the top is golden and the cheese is bubbly.
6. Garnish with fresh cilantro before serving.

Chicken and Corn Chili

Ingredients:

- 2 cups cooked and shredded chicken
- 1 can corn kernels, drained
- 1 can diced tomatoes
- 1 onion, chopped
- 2 cloves garlic, minced
- 1 tbsp chili powder
- 1 tsp cumin
- 4 cups chicken broth
- Salt and pepper to taste
- Fresh cilantro for garnish

Instructions:

1. In a large pot, sauté onions and garlic until soft.
2. Add the shredded chicken, corn, diced tomatoes, chili powder, cumin, chicken broth, salt, and pepper.
3. Bring to a boil, then reduce the heat and simmer for 25-30 minutes.
4. Garnish with fresh cilantro and serve with tortilla chips or cornbread.

Mexican Chicken and Avocado Salad

Ingredients:

- 2 cups cooked and shredded chicken
- 1 avocado, diced
- 1 cup corn kernels (fresh or frozen)
- 1/2 cup black beans, drained and rinsed
- 1/2 cup diced tomatoes
- 1/4 cup red onion, chopped
- 1/4 cup fresh cilantro, chopped
- 2 tbsp lime juice
- Salt and pepper to taste

Instructions:

1. In a large bowl, combine shredded chicken, avocado, corn, black beans, tomatoes, onion, and cilantro.
2. Drizzle with lime juice and season with salt and pepper.
3. Toss everything together and serve as a refreshing, healthy meal or side dish.

Chicken Empanadas with Salsa Verde

Ingredients:

- **For the Empanadas:**
    - 2 cups cooked and shredded chicken
    - 1/2 cup diced onion
    - 1/4 cup diced bell pepper
    - 1/4 cup tomato paste
    - 1/2 tsp cumin
    - 1/4 tsp paprika
    - Salt and pepper to taste
    - 1 package empanada dough (or homemade dough)
    - 1 egg (for egg wash)
- **For the Salsa Verde:**
    - 1 lb tomatillos, husked and rinsed
    - 2 cloves garlic
    - 1/2 cup cilantro leaves
    - 1/2 tsp lime juice
    - Salt to taste

Instructions:

1. **For the Empanadas:**
    - Preheat the oven to 375°F (190°C).
    - In a skillet, sauté onions and bell peppers until softened. Add the tomato paste, cumin, paprika, salt, and pepper, and cook for 2-3 minutes.
    - Stir in the shredded chicken and cook for another 5 minutes.
    - Roll out the empanada dough and spoon the chicken mixture onto each circle. Fold the dough over and crimp the edges to seal. Brush with the beaten egg.
    - Bake for 20 minutes, or until golden brown.
2. **For the Salsa Verde:**
    - In a saucepan, simmer tomatillos and garlic for 10-15 minutes until soft.
    - Blend the tomatillos, garlic, cilantro, lime juice, and salt until smooth.
    - Serve the empanadas with the salsa verde for dipping.

Baked Chicken with Mexican Spices

Ingredients:

- 4 chicken breasts or thighs
- 2 tbsp olive oil
- 1 tbsp chili powder
- 1 tsp cumin
- 1 tsp paprika
- 1/2 tsp garlic powder
- 1/2 tsp onion powder
- 1/2 tsp salt
- 1/4 tsp black pepper
- 1 lime, cut into wedges

Instructions:

1. Preheat the oven to 400°F (200°C).
2. In a small bowl, mix chili powder, cumin, paprika, garlic powder, onion powder, salt, and pepper.
3. Rub the chicken pieces with olive oil and then coat with the spice mixture.
4. Place the chicken on a baking sheet and bake for 25-30 minutes, or until the chicken is fully cooked and the juices run clear.
5. Squeeze lime wedges over the chicken before serving.

Chicken and Bean Burritos

Ingredients:

- 2 cups cooked and shredded chicken
- 1 cup refried beans
- 8 flour tortillas
- 1 cup shredded cheese
- 1/2 cup salsa
- 1/4 cup sour cream
- Fresh cilantro for garnish

Instructions:

1. Warm the tortillas in a skillet or microwave.
2. Spread a thin layer of refried beans on each tortilla.
3. Add the shredded chicken and top with cheese.
4. Roll up the tortillas and place them seam side down in a baking dish.
5. Pour salsa over the top and bake at 375°F (190°C) for 15-20 minutes or until the cheese is melted.
6. Serve with sour cream and fresh cilantro.

Pollo en Salsa Roja

Ingredients:

- 4 chicken thighs or breasts
- 2 cups canned tomato sauce
- 1 onion, chopped
- 2 cloves garlic, minced
- 1-2 dried guajillo chiles, seeds removed
- 1 tsp cumin
- 1/2 tsp oregano
- Salt and pepper to taste
- 1 tbsp olive oil

Instructions:

1. In a dry skillet, toast the guajillo chiles for a minute until fragrant, then rehydrate them in hot water for 10 minutes.
2. Blend the chiles with tomato sauce, onion, garlic, cumin, oregano, salt, and pepper until smooth.
3. In a large pan, heat olive oil and brown the chicken on both sides.
4. Pour the salsa roja over the chicken and simmer for 25-30 minutes, or until the chicken is fully cooked.
5. Serve with rice or tortillas.

Chicken Fajita Skillet

Ingredients:

- 2 chicken breasts, thinly sliced
- 1 bell pepper, thinly sliced
- 1 onion, thinly sliced
- 1 tbsp olive oil
- 1 tsp chili powder
- 1 tsp cumin
- 1/2 tsp paprika
- 1/4 tsp garlic powder
- Salt and pepper to taste
- Tortillas, for serving
- Lime wedges and cilantro for garnish

Instructions:

1. In a large skillet, heat olive oil over medium-high heat.
2. Add the sliced chicken, bell pepper, and onion. Season with chili powder, cumin, paprika, garlic powder, salt, and pepper.
3. Cook for 7-10 minutes, stirring occasionally, until the chicken is cooked through and the vegetables are tender.
4. Serve the fajita mixture with warm tortillas and garnish with lime wedges and cilantro.

Chicken and Zucchini Tacos

Ingredients:

- 2 cups cooked and shredded chicken
- 1 zucchini, grated
- 1 tbsp olive oil
- 1 tsp cumin
- 1/2 tsp chili powder
- Salt and pepper to taste
- 8 small corn tortillas
- Fresh salsa, for topping
- Fresh cilantro for garnish
- Lime wedges for serving

Instructions:

1. In a skillet, heat olive oil over medium heat. Add the grated zucchini and sauté for 3-5 minutes until tender.
2. Stir in the shredded chicken, cumin, chili powder, salt, and pepper. Cook for another 2-3 minutes.
3. Warm the tortillas in a skillet or microwave.
4. Spoon the chicken and zucchini mixture into each tortilla.
5. Top with fresh salsa and cilantro, and serve with lime wedges.

Baked Chicken with Mole Sauce

Ingredients:

- 4 chicken breasts or thighs
- 1 cup mole sauce (store-bought or homemade)
- 1 tbsp olive oil
- 1 tsp cumin
- 1/2 tsp cinnamon
- 1 tbsp sesame seeds (for garnish)
- Fresh cilantro for garnish

Instructions:

1. Preheat the oven to 375°F (190°C).
2. Rub the chicken with olive oil, cumin, and cinnamon.
3. In a baking dish, pour the mole sauce over the chicken, making sure it's well-coated.
4. Cover the dish with foil and bake for 35-40 minutes or until the chicken is fully cooked.
5. Garnish with sesame seeds and fresh cilantro before serving.

Chicken Chile Rellenos Casserole

Ingredients:

- 2 cups cooked and shredded chicken
- 4 poblano peppers, roasted, peeled, and chopped
- 1 cup shredded cheese (cheddar, Monterrey jack, or a mix)
- 1/2 cup onion, chopped
- 1/2 cup sour cream
- 1/2 cup milk
- 3 large eggs
- 1 tsp cumin
- Salt and pepper to taste
- 1/4 cup cilantro for garnish

Instructions:

1. Preheat the oven to 375°F (190°C).
2. In a large bowl, whisk together the eggs, milk, sour cream, cumin, salt, and pepper.
3. Stir in the shredded chicken, roasted poblano peppers, onion, and 1/2 of the cheese.
4. Pour the mixture into a greased casserole dish and top with the remaining cheese.
5. Bake for 30-35 minutes until set and golden brown.
6. Garnish with cilantro before serving.

Chicken and Spinach Enchiladas

Ingredients:

- 2 cups cooked and shredded chicken
- 1 cup spinach, chopped
- 1/2 cup onion, chopped
- 1 can (10 oz) red enchilada sauce
- 8 corn tortillas
- 1 cup shredded cheese (cheddar or Monterrey jack)
- 1 tbsp olive oil
- Salt and pepper to taste

Instructions:

1. Preheat the oven to 375°F (190°C).
2. In a skillet, heat olive oil over medium heat and sauté onions until soft. Add spinach and cook until wilted. Stir in the shredded chicken and season with salt and pepper.
3. Warm the tortillas and spoon the chicken mixture onto each tortilla. Roll them up and place them seam-side down in a baking dish.
4. Pour the enchilada sauce over the tortillas and top with shredded cheese.
5. Bake for 20-25 minutes until bubbly and golden.

Pollo en Salsa de Tamarindo (Tamarind Chicken)

Ingredients:

- 4 chicken breasts or thighs
- 1/2 cup tamarind paste
- 1/4 cup brown sugar
- 1/2 cup orange juice
- 1/2 tsp cumin
- 1/4 tsp chili powder
- Salt and pepper to taste
- 1 tbsp olive oil
- Fresh cilantro for garnish

Instructions:

1. In a bowl, whisk together the tamarind paste, brown sugar, orange juice, cumin, chili powder, salt, and pepper.
2. Heat olive oil in a skillet over medium-high heat. Brown the chicken on both sides for 5-6 minutes.
3. Pour the tamarind sauce over the chicken, reduce heat, and simmer for 15-20 minutes until the chicken is fully cooked.
4. Garnish with fresh cilantro and serve with rice or tortillas.

Chicken Salsas with Tortillas

Ingredients:

- 2 cups cooked and shredded chicken
- 1/2 cup salsa roja
- 1/2 cup salsa verde
- 8 small corn tortillas
- 1/2 cup shredded cheese (optional)
- Fresh cilantro for garnish
- Lime wedges for serving

Instructions:

1. Warm the tortillas in a skillet or microwave.
2. In a bowl, combine the shredded chicken with both the salsa roja and salsa verde.
3. Spoon the chicken mixture onto each tortilla, sprinkle with cheese if using, and garnish with cilantro.
4. Serve with lime wedges for a zesty touch.

Chicken and Pineapple Tacos

Ingredients:

- 2 cups cooked and shredded chicken
- 1/2 cup diced pineapple
- 1/4 cup red onion, finely chopped
- 1 tbsp lime juice
- 1 tsp chili powder
- 1/2 tsp cumin
- 1/4 tsp smoked paprika
- Salt and pepper to taste
- 8 small corn tortillas
- Fresh cilantro for garnish

Instructions:

1. In a bowl, combine the shredded chicken, diced pineapple, red onion, lime juice, chili powder, cumin, smoked paprika, salt, and pepper.
2. Warm the tortillas in a skillet or microwave.
3. Spoon the chicken and pineapple mixture onto each tortilla.
4. Garnish with fresh cilantro and serve with extra lime wedges.

Chicken Taco Salad

Ingredients:

- 2 cups cooked and shredded chicken
- 4 cups mixed lettuce or greens
- 1/2 cup diced tomatoes
- 1/2 cup corn kernels
- 1/4 cup black beans, rinsed and drained
- 1/2 cup shredded cheese
- 1/4 cup sour cream
- 2 tbsp salsa
- 1 tbsp olive oil
- 1 tsp chili powder
- Salt and pepper to taste

Instructions:

1. In a large bowl, toss together the greens, diced tomatoes, corn, black beans, and shredded chicken.
2. Drizzle olive oil, sprinkle with chili powder, salt, and pepper, and toss again.
3. Serve the salad topped with cheese, sour cream, and salsa.
4. Optional: Serve with tortilla chips for added crunch.

www.ingramcontent.com/pod-product-compliance
Lightning Source LLC
LaVergne TN
LVHW081342060526
838201LV00055B/2798